DRUNK SANTA
& THE NAUGHTY ELVES
Christmas Coloring Book For Adults

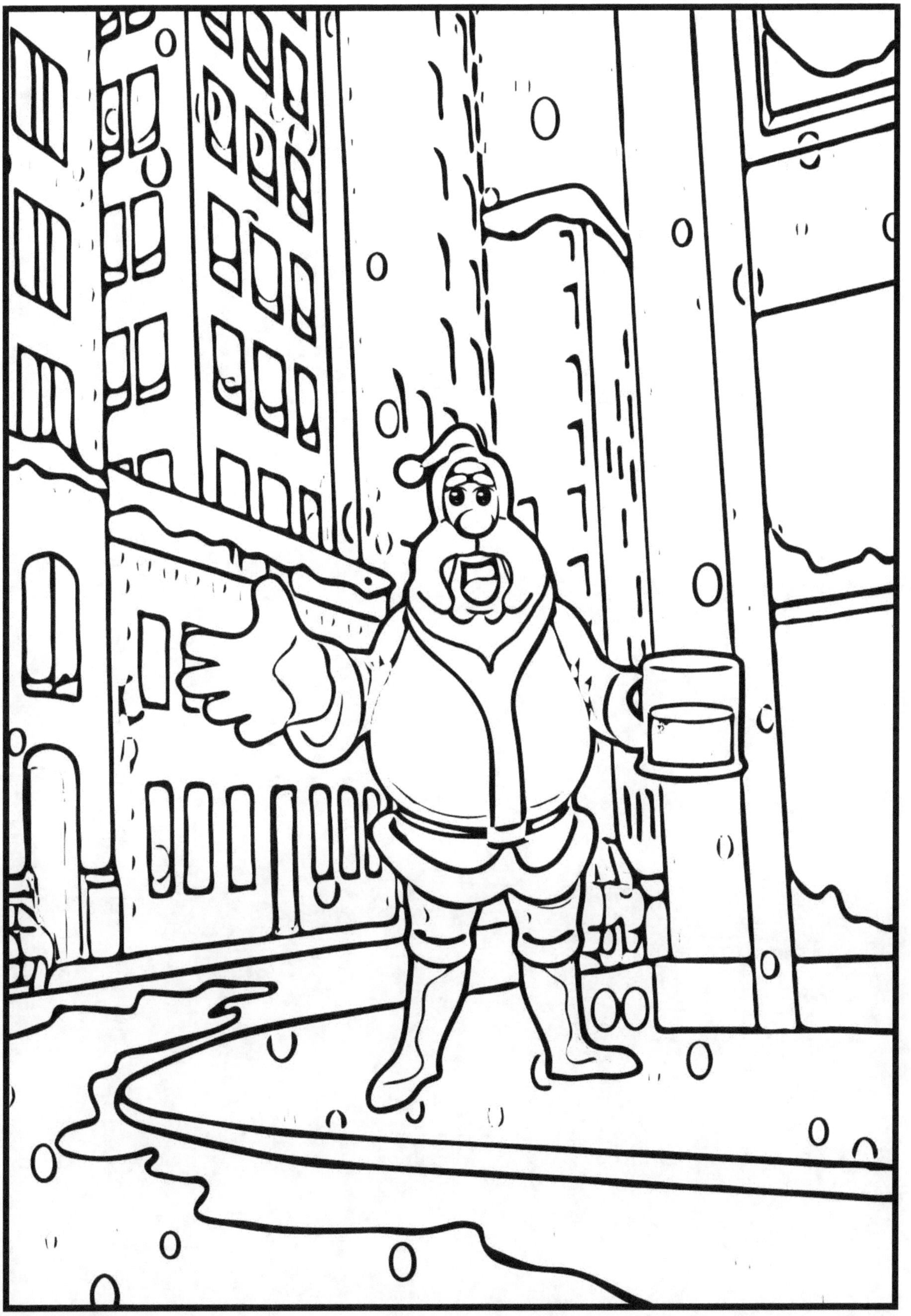

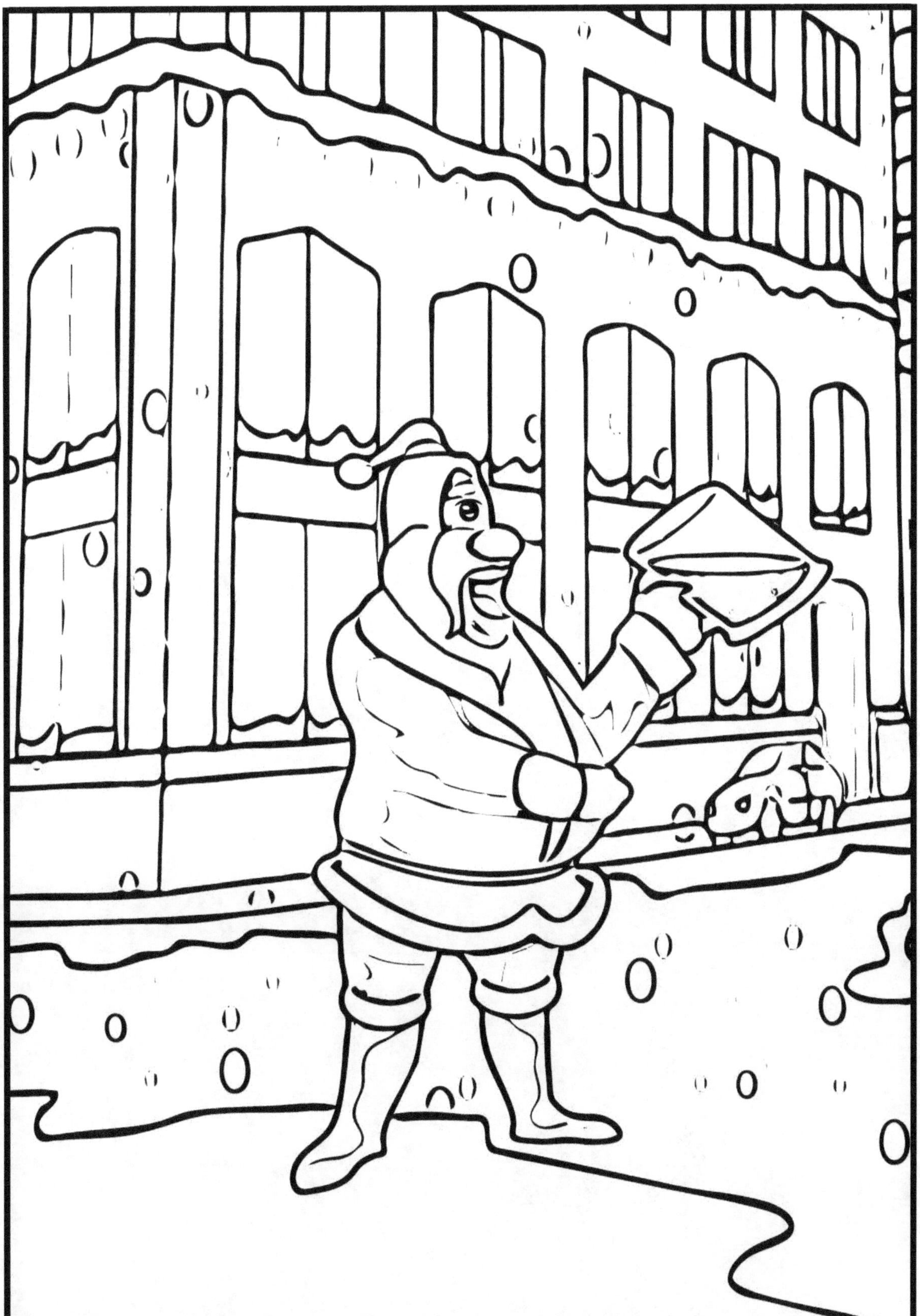

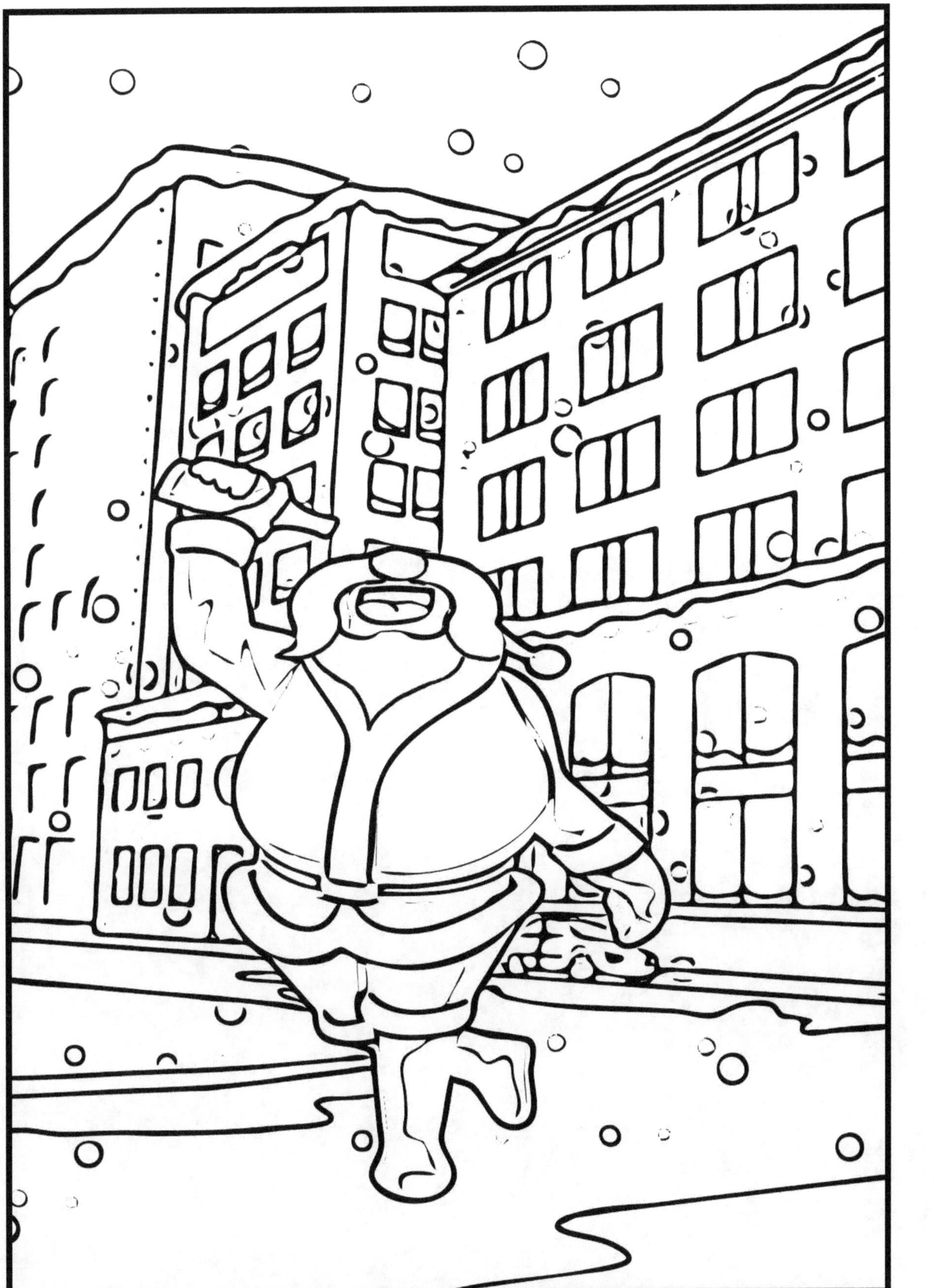

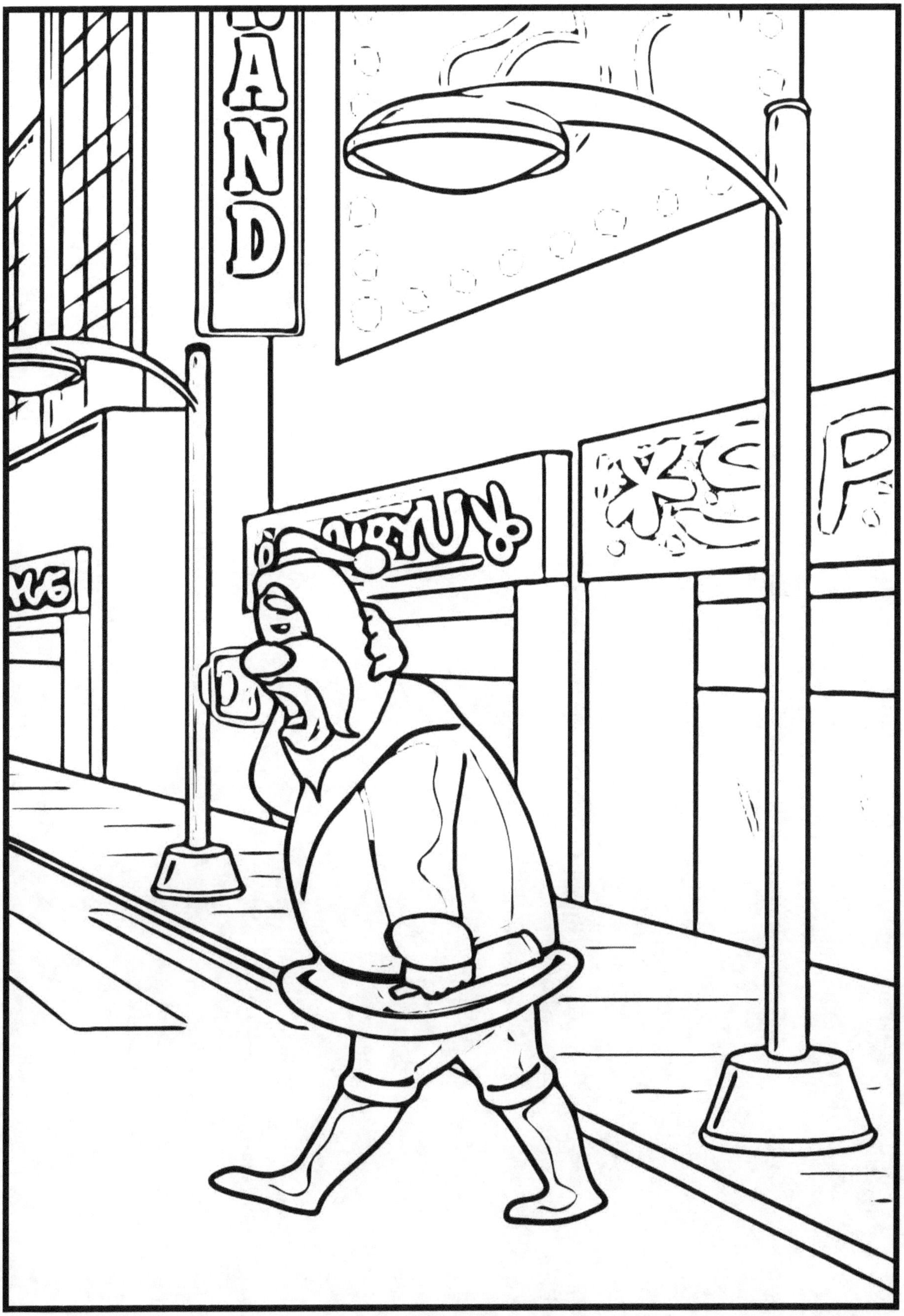
AND

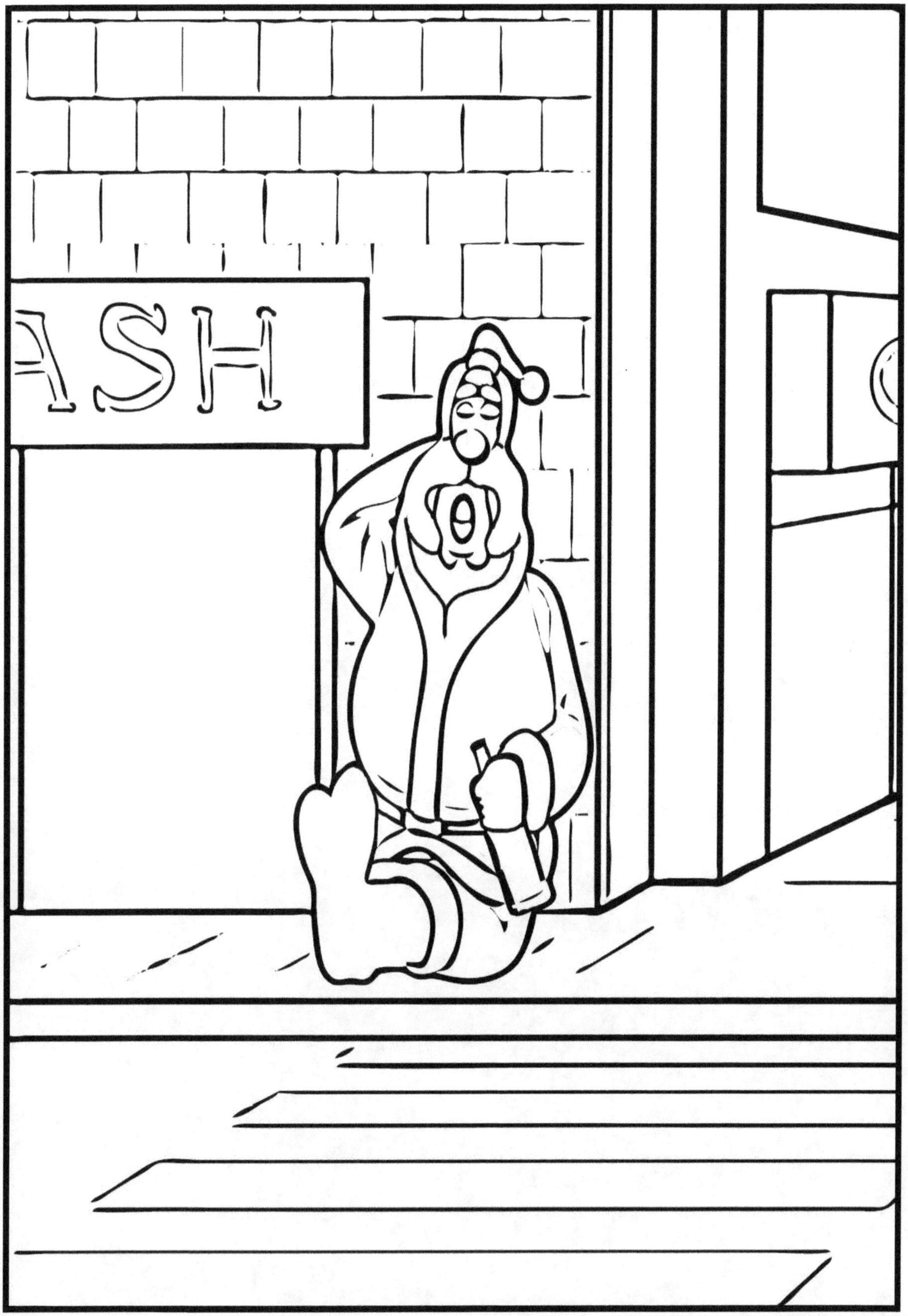
ASH

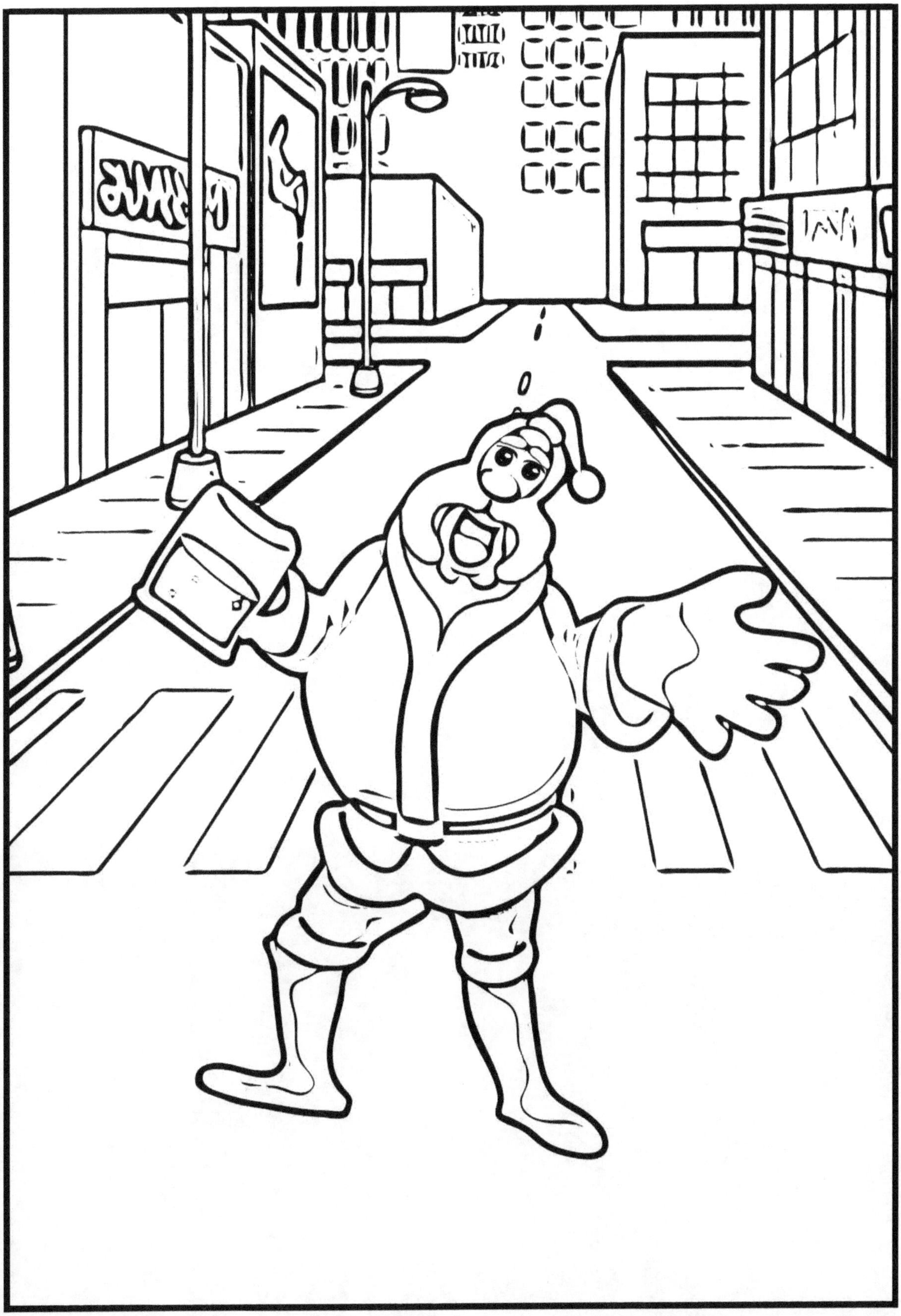

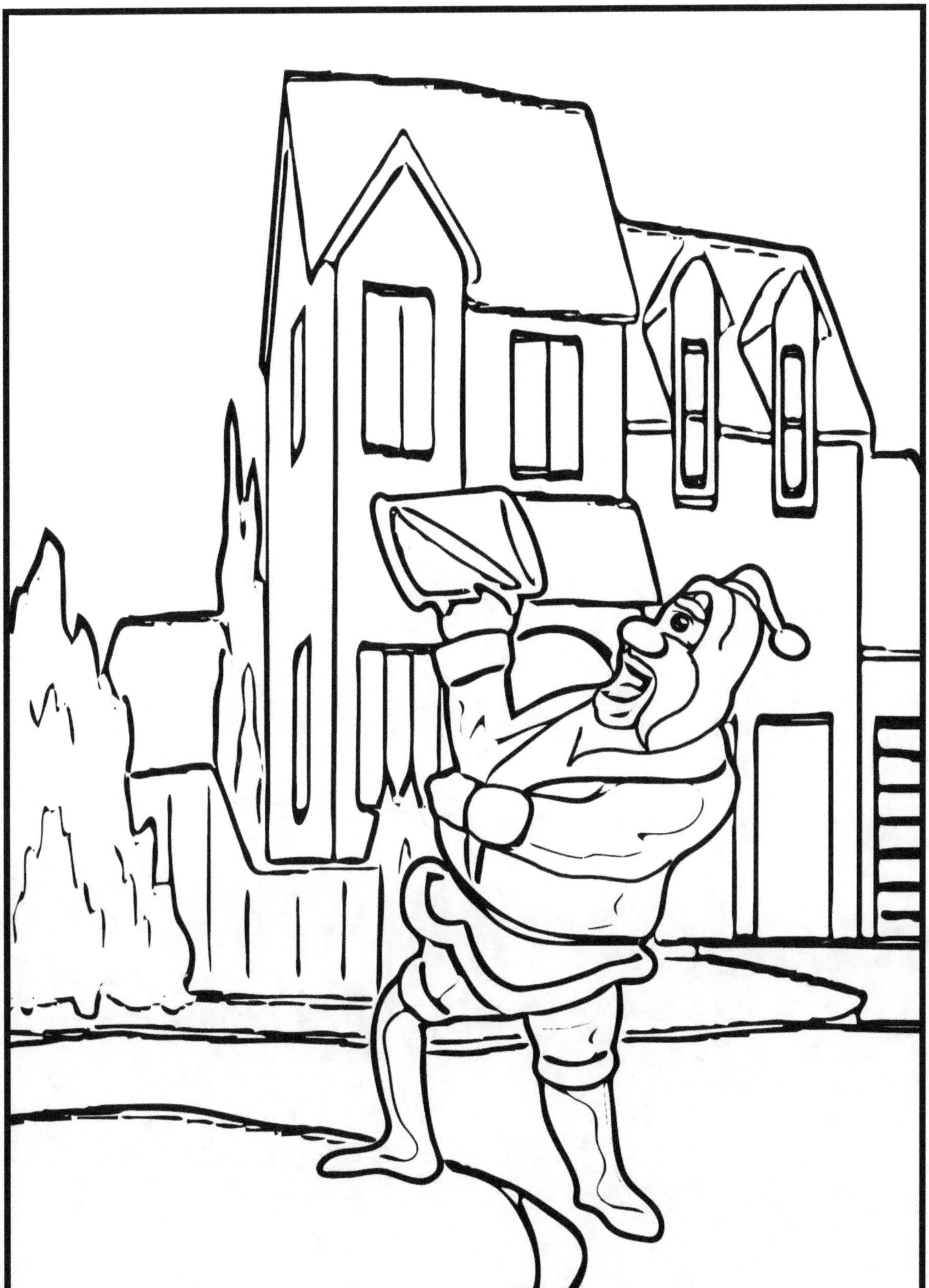

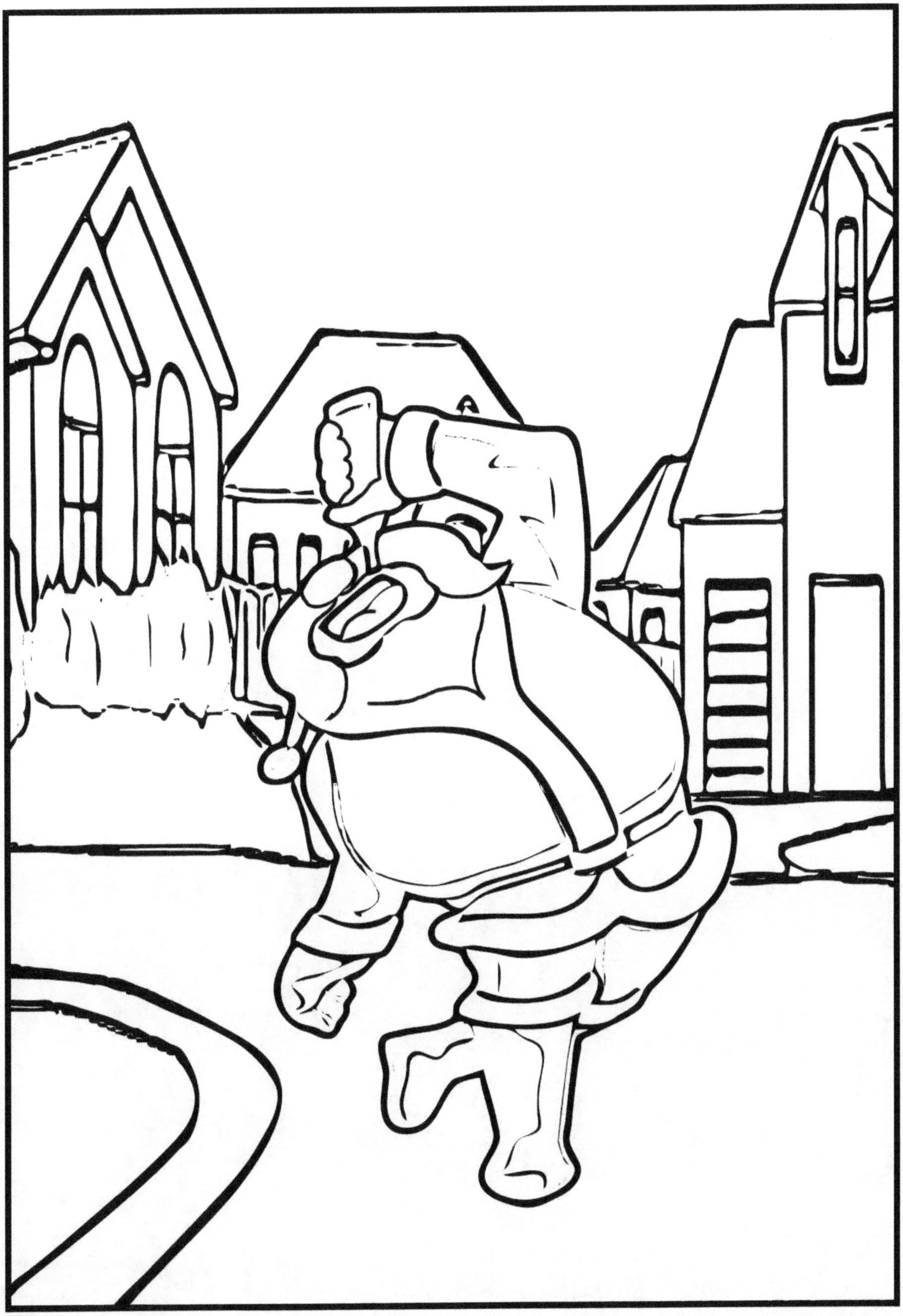

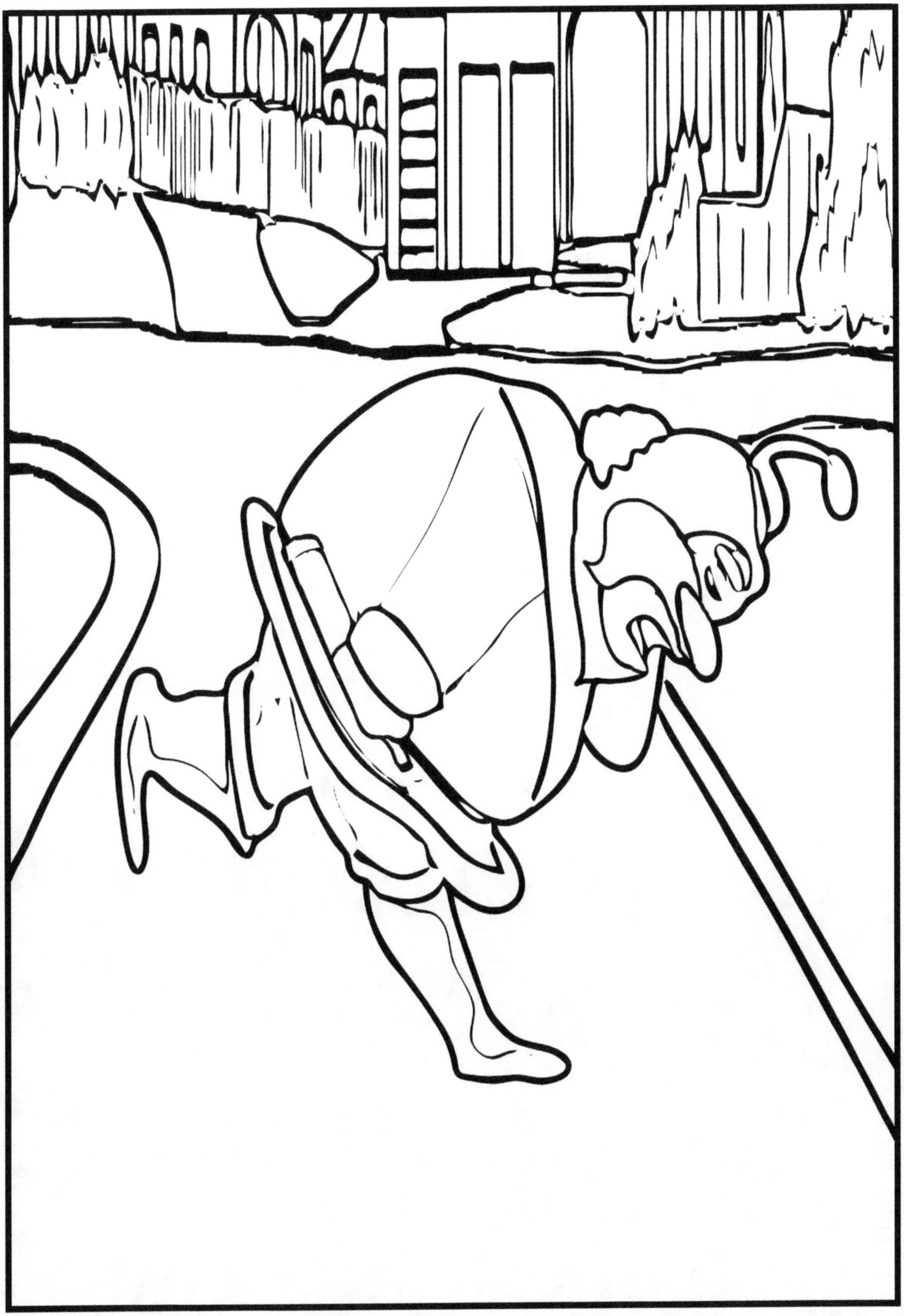

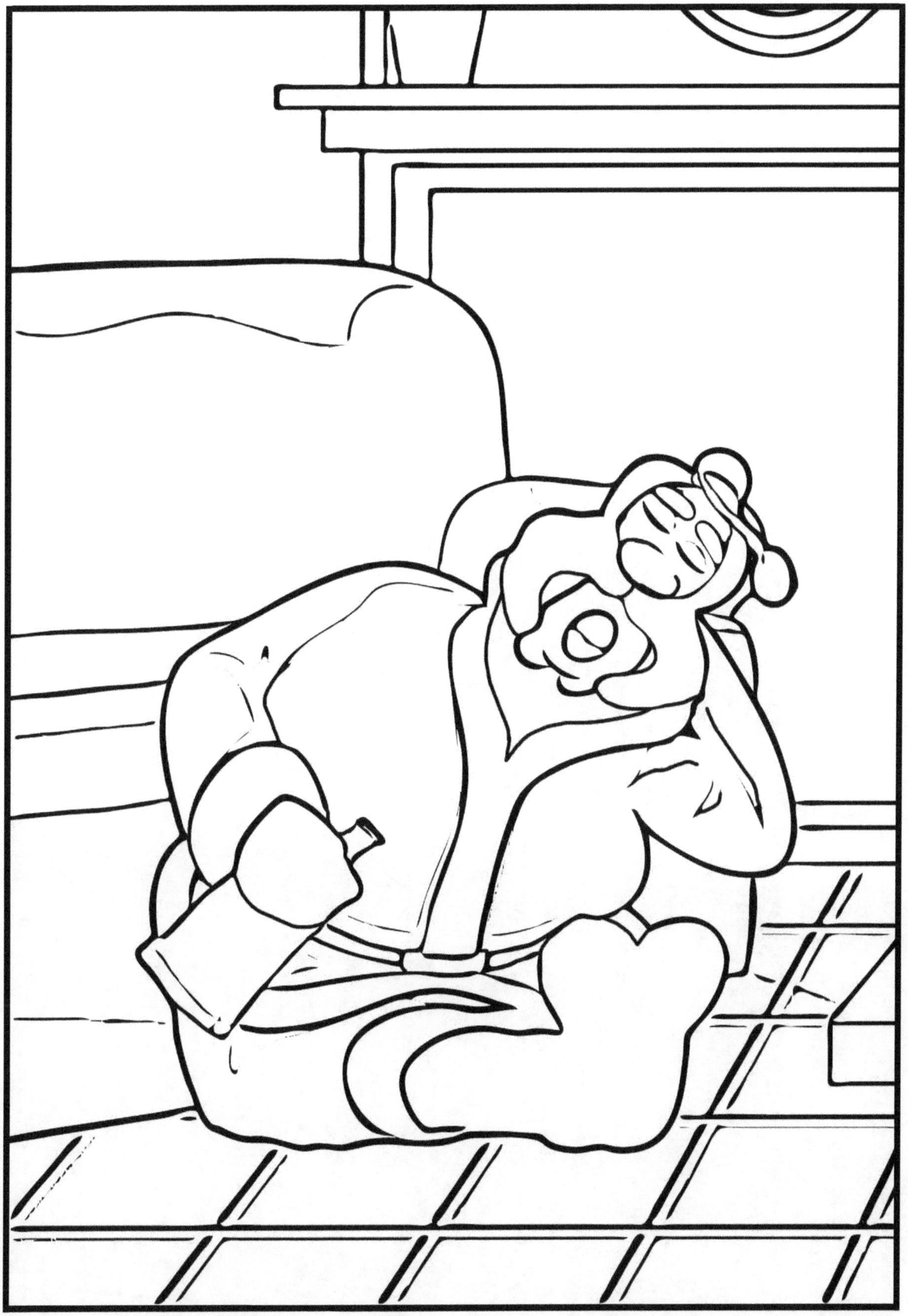

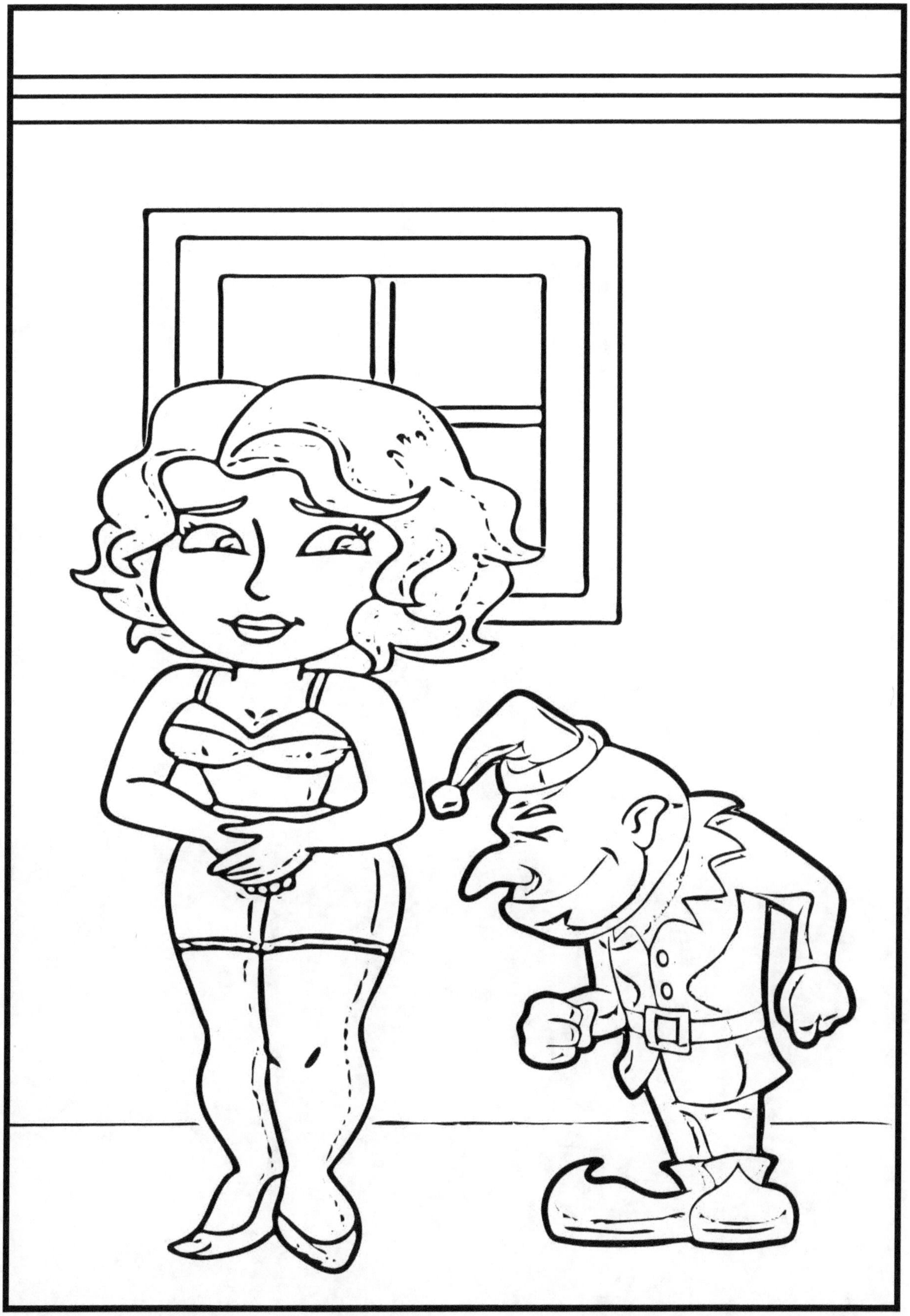

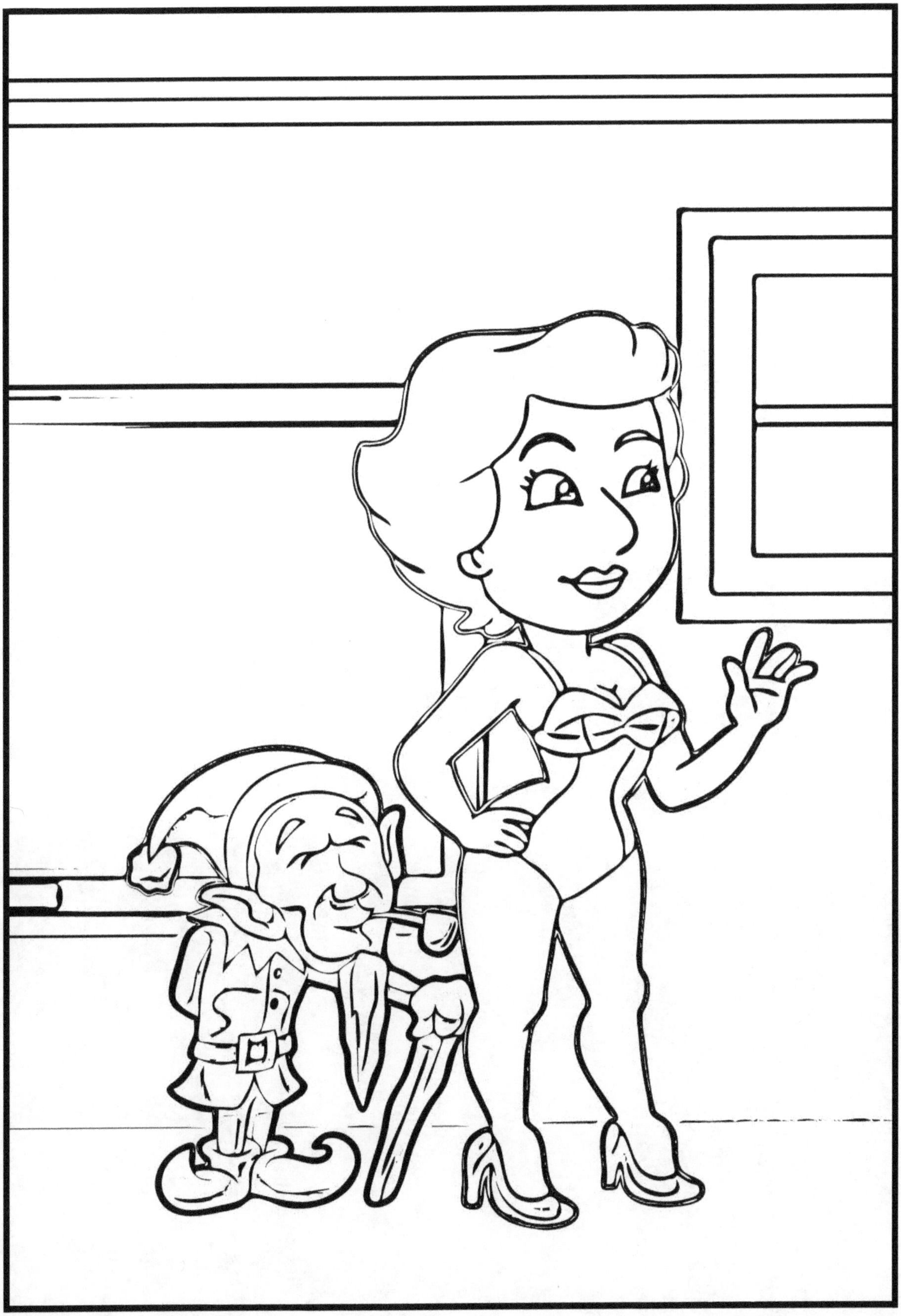

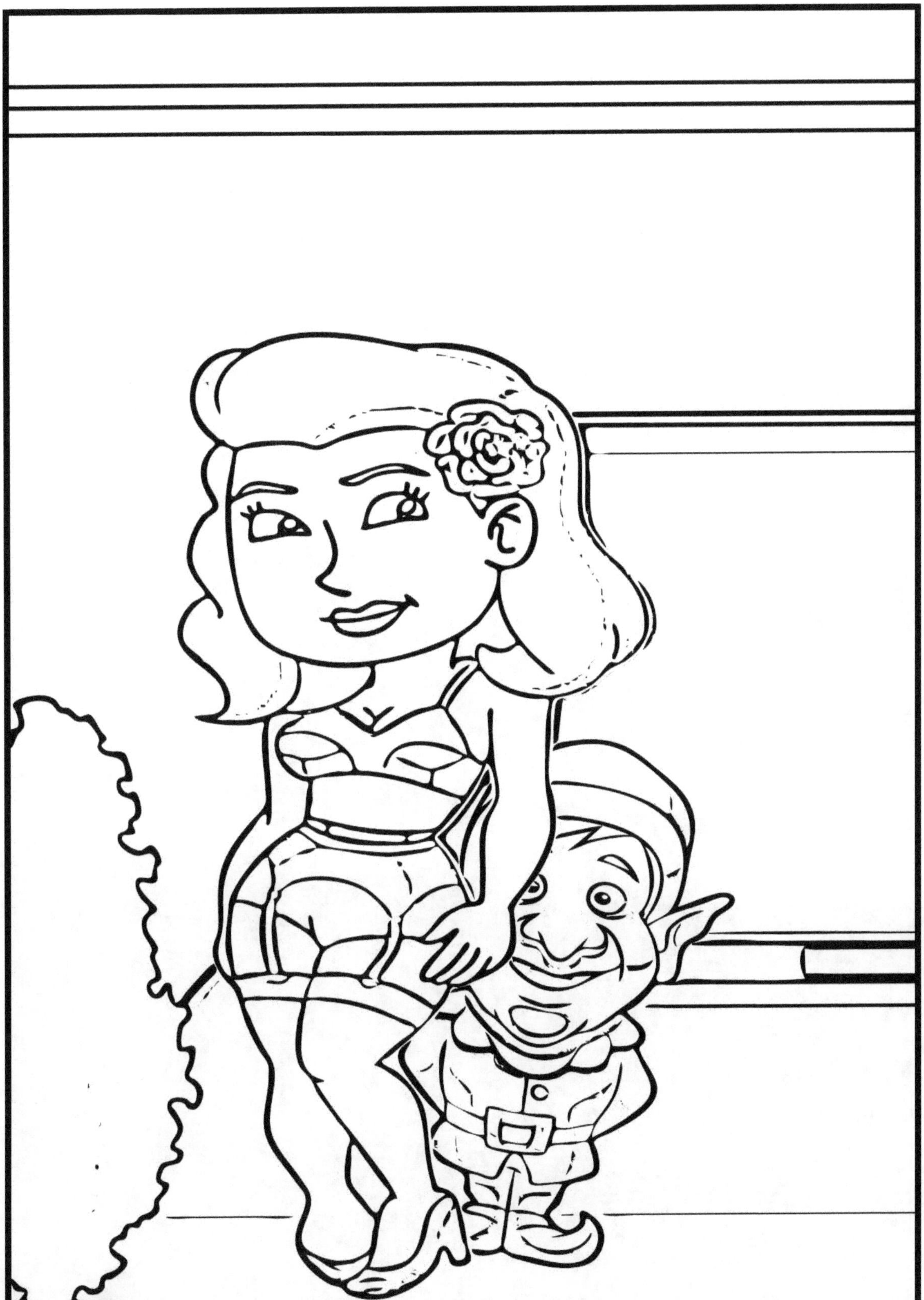

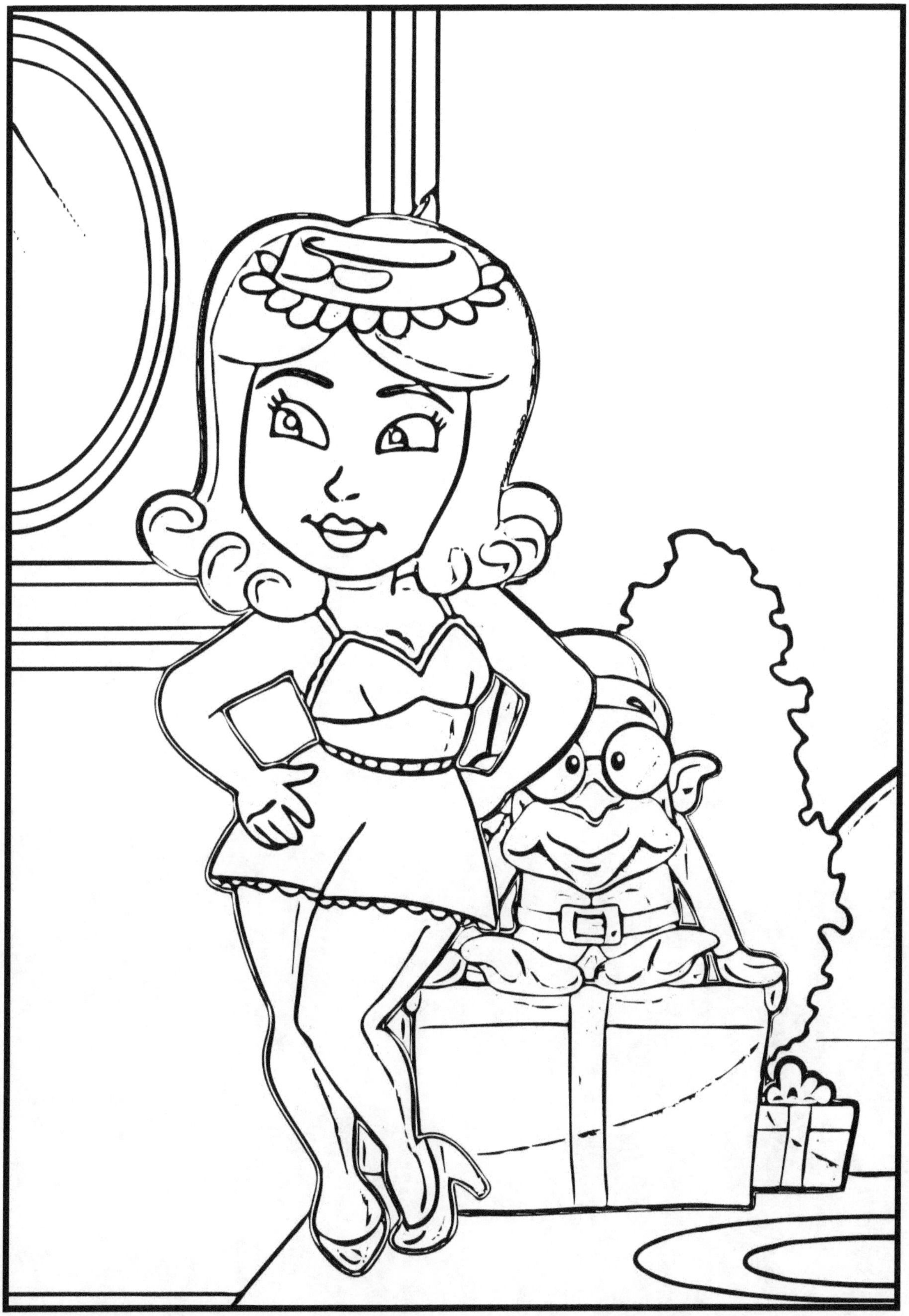

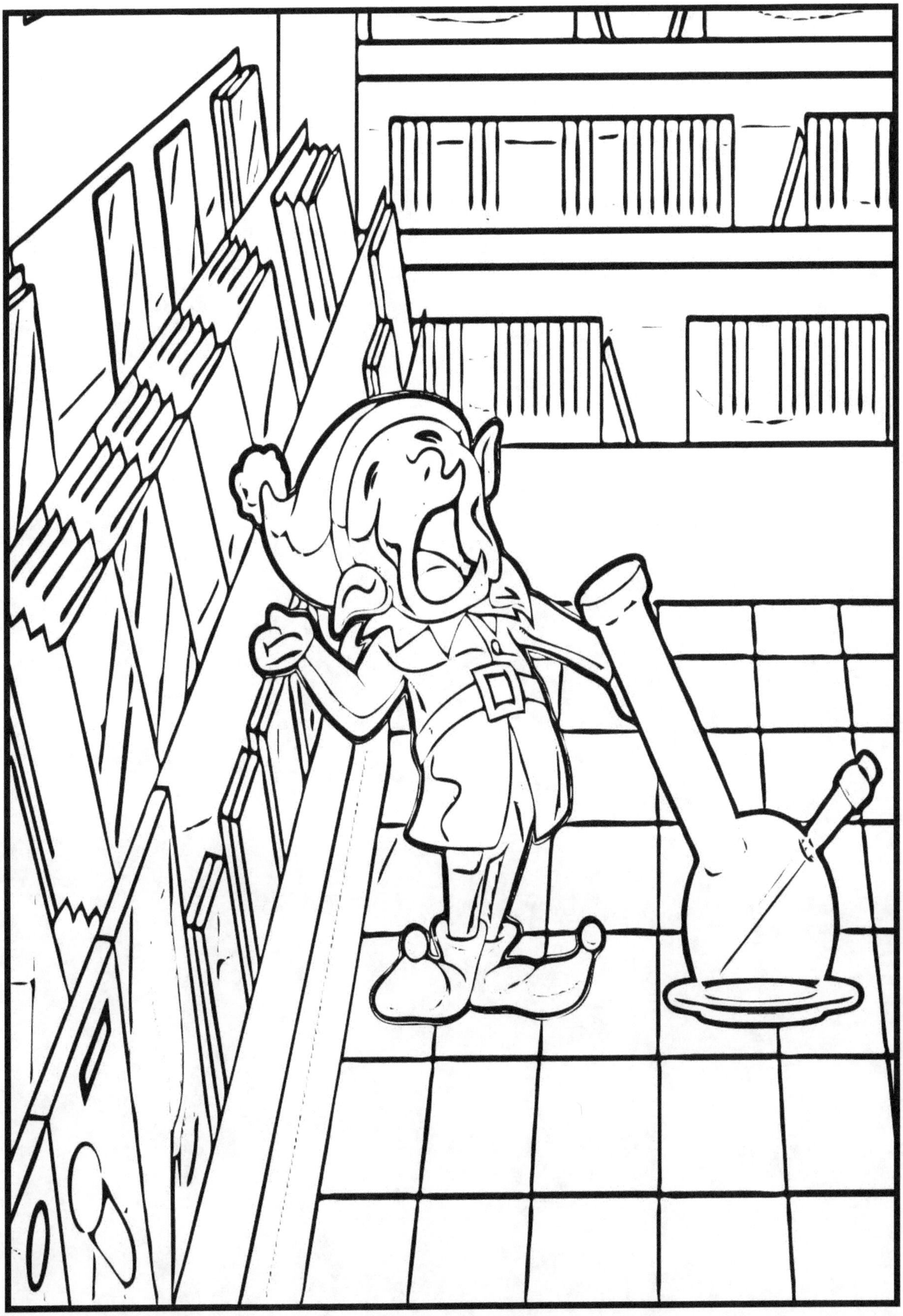

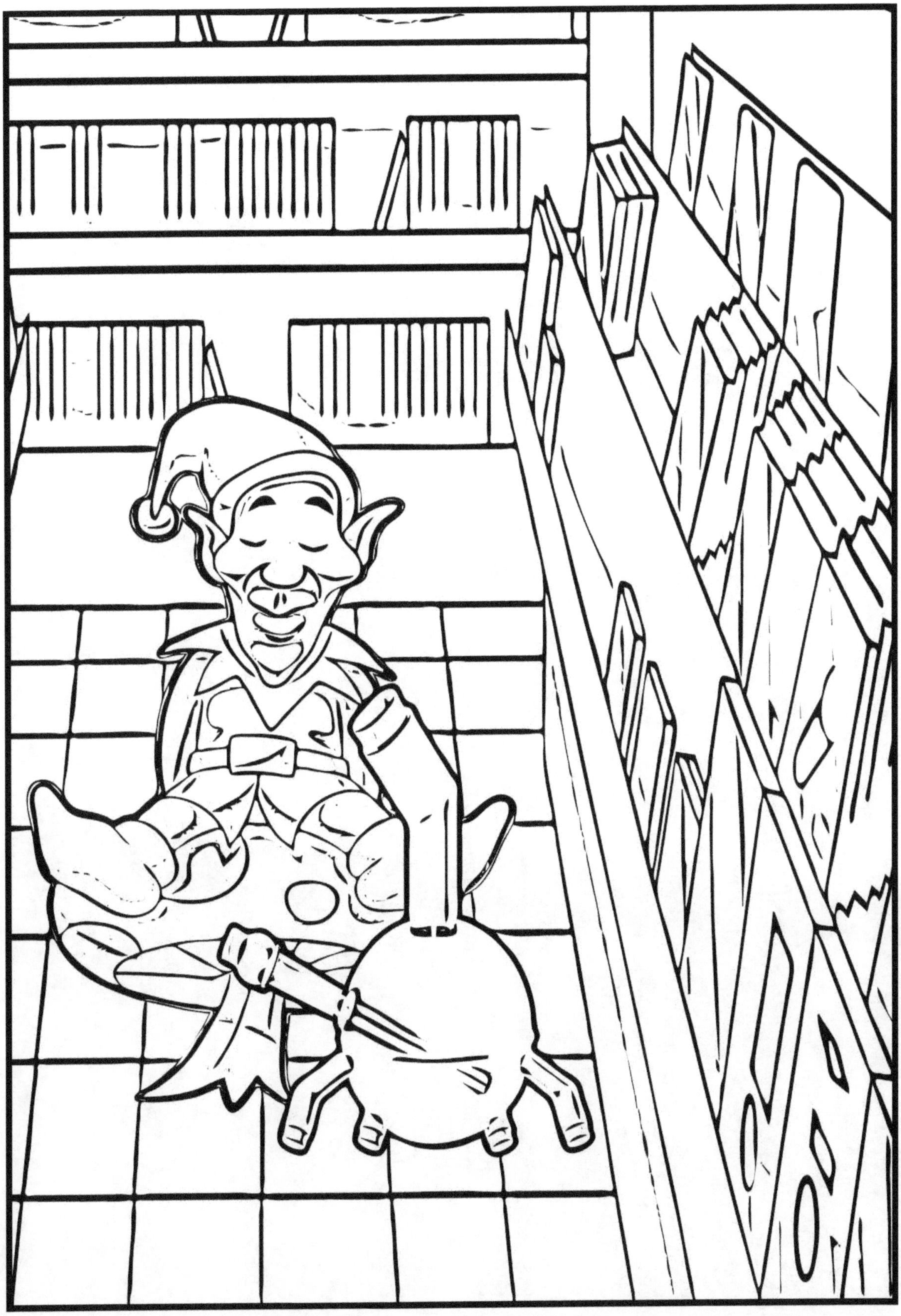

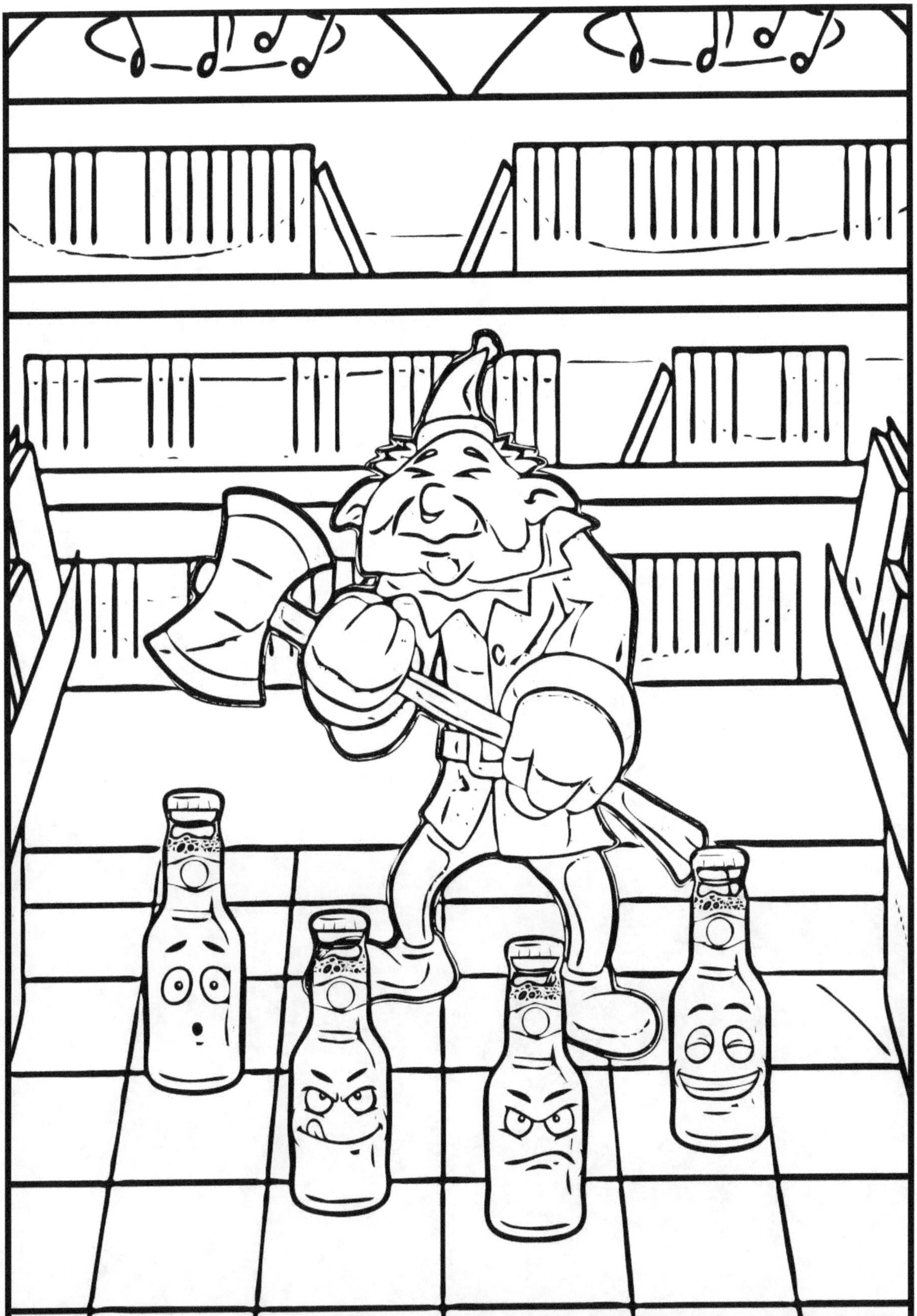

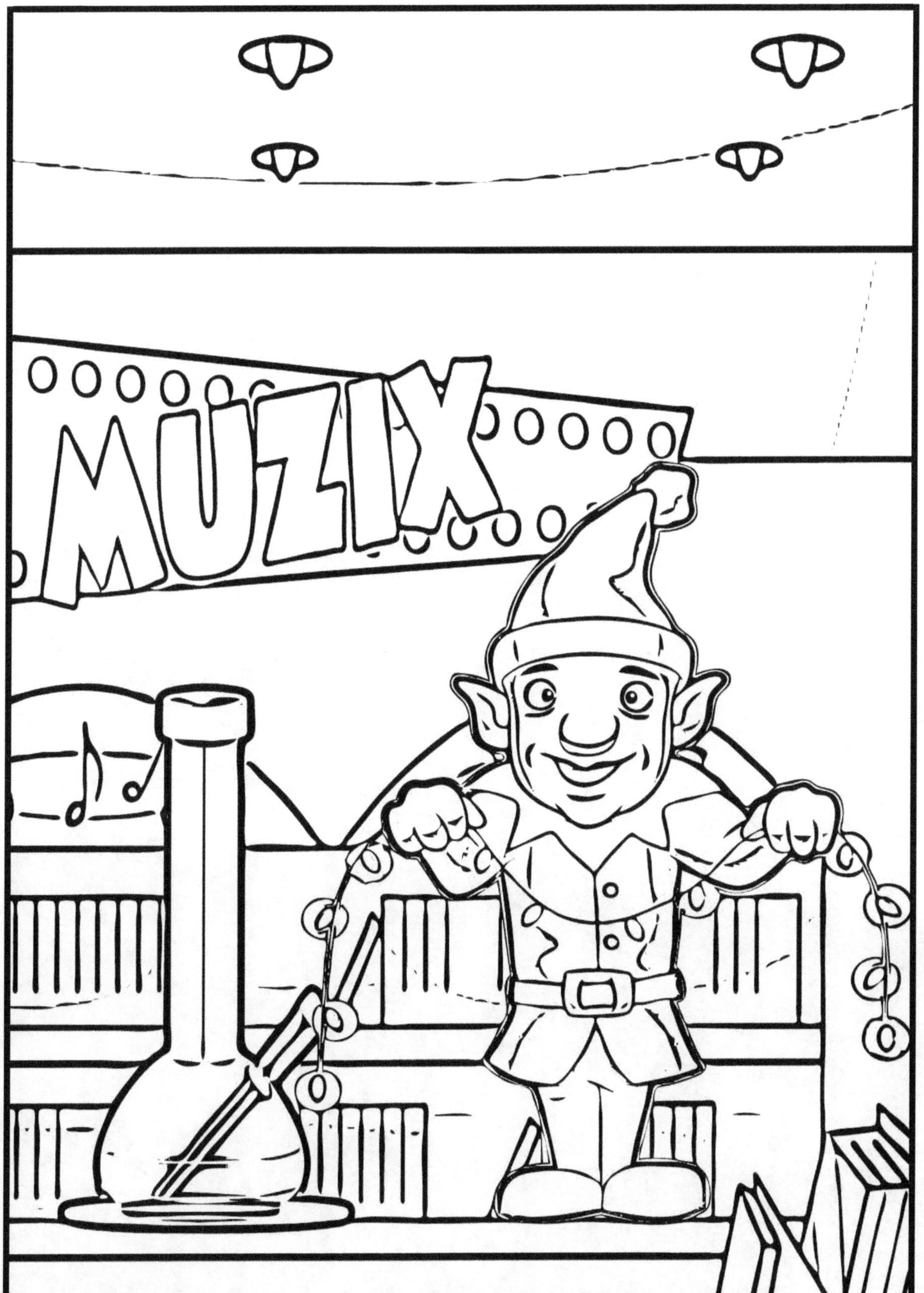
MUZIX

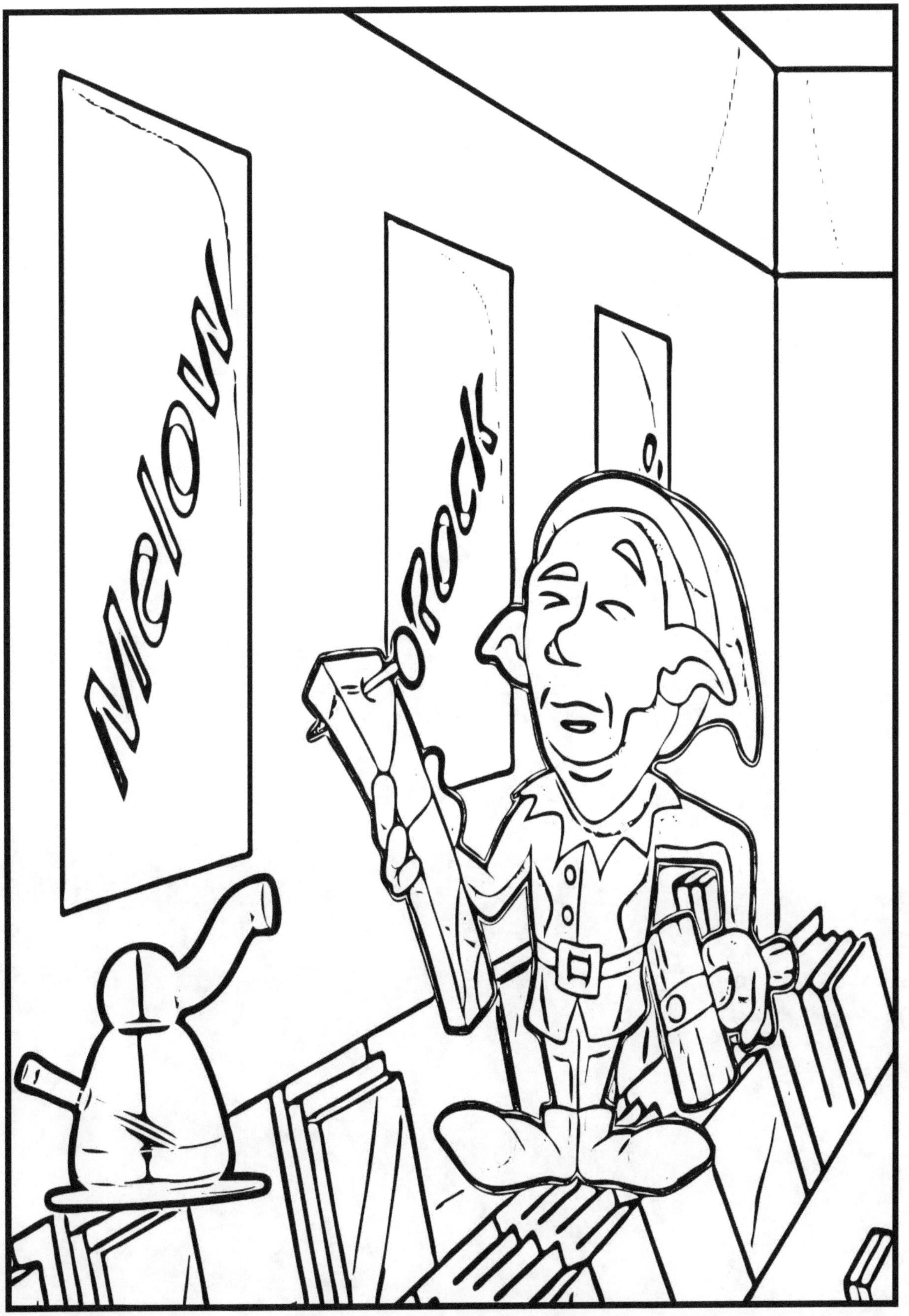

Mellow
Rock

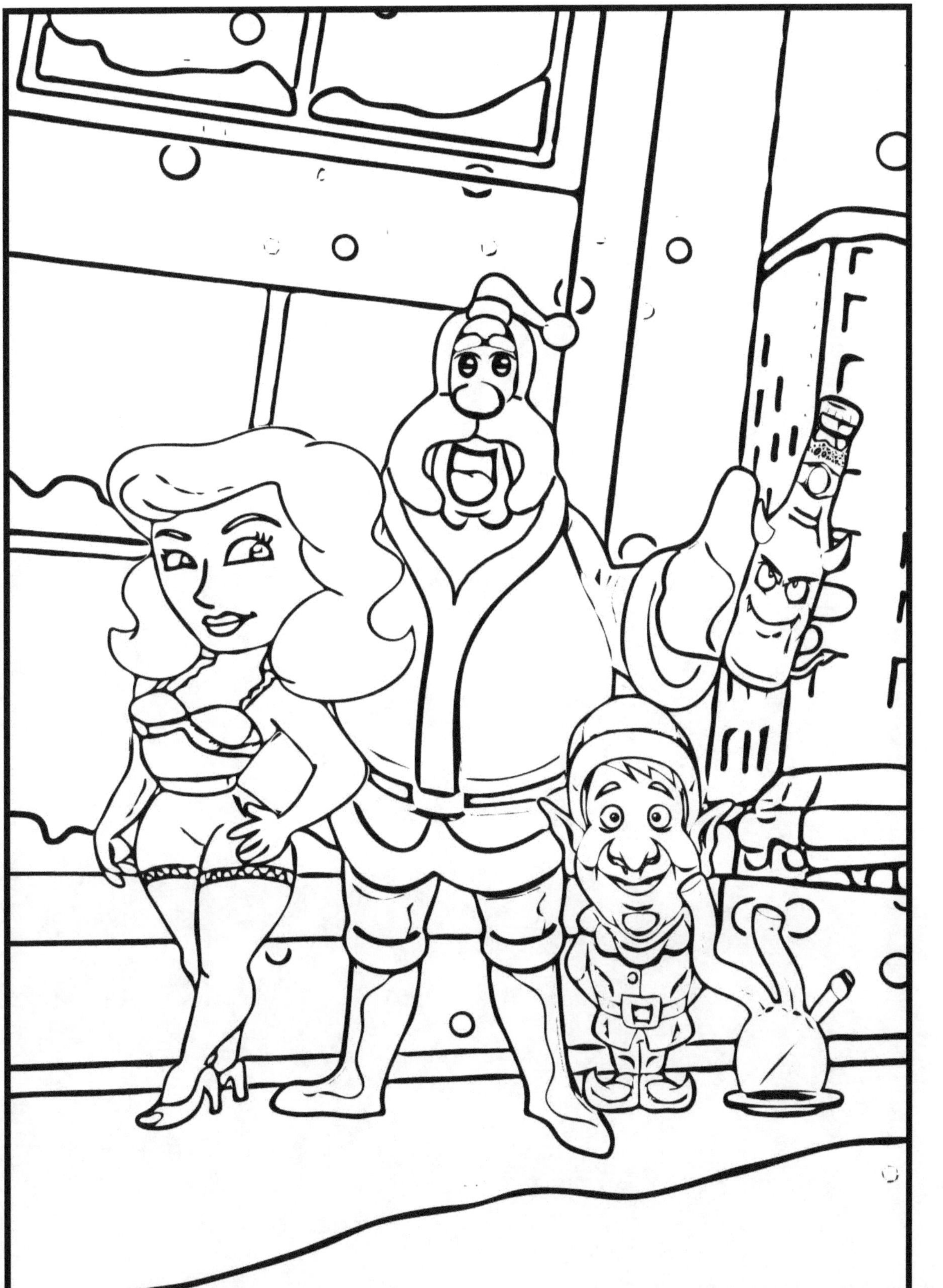

www.ingramcontent.com/pod-product-compliance
Lightning Source LLC
Chambersburg PA
CBHW080617180526
45168CB00007B/2956